THE GREATEST FEARS

Horrible HOMES

BookLife RAPID Readers

BookLife
PUBLISHING

©2023
BookLife Publishing Ltd.
King's Lynn, Norfolk
PE30 4LS, UK

All rights reserved.
Printed in China.

A catalogue record for this book is available from the British Library.

ISBN: 978-1-80505-028-5

Written by:
John Wood
Adapted by:
Noah Leatherland
Edited by:
Kirsty Holmes
Designed by:
Jasmine Pointer

FSC
www.fsc.org
MIX
Paper from responsible sources
FSC® C113515

All facts, statistics, web addresses and URLs in this book were verified as valid and accurate at time of writing.
No responsibility for any changes to external websites or references can be accepted by either the author or publisher.

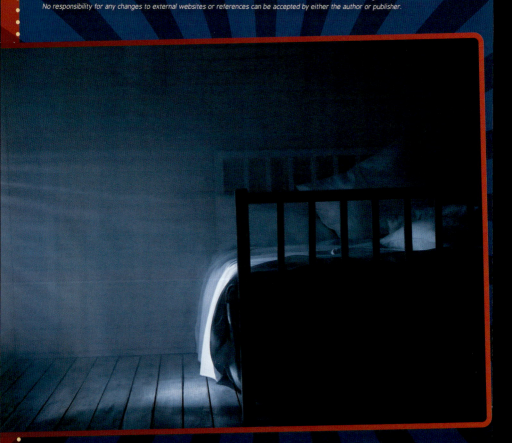

Photo Credits

Images are courtesy of Shutterstock.com. With thanks to Getty Images, Thinkstock Photo and iStockphoto.
RECURRING – pikepicture, kantimar kongjaidee, MagicMary. COVER – Mariusz Lopusiewicz, XONIX, jenny on the moon, M_Videous, Tornado design, logistock, Tuleedin, Sudowoodo, ansveta, vladwel, ToeyFatboy. 4–5 – Robie Online, sicegame. 6–7 – Vasilyev Alexandr, Nick Fedirko, ysclips design. 8–9 – Christopher Edwin Nuzzaco, Fer Gregory, Telman Bagirov. 10–11 – Qvils, Master1305. 12–13 – Atlantic Records(Life time: Published before 1978 without a copyright notice), Public domain, via Wikimedia Commons, Stefano Chiacchiarini '74, aappp, Gwens Graphic Studio. 14–15 – Thomas La Mela, Andrew Lever, Who If Not Us. 16–17 – Jirik V, Andrey_Popov, Natty_Blissful, maryartist. 18–19 – Juta, Galleria Laureata, Tupungato. 20–21 – Asier Romero, Janis M Bock, zef art, Nsit, Vitvider. 22–23 – CLIPAREA l Custom media, Maksym Drozd, Cookie Studio, Vitalii Petrenko.24–25 – mizar_21984, Elnur, Roi and Roi. 26–27 – sirtravelalot, GoodStudio, Cast Of Thousands, Qualit Design. 28–29 – Beata Gabryelska, MarinaP.

CONTENTS

Words that look like *this* are explained in the glossary on page 31.

Page 4 Welcome to the Show!
Page 6 Creepy Sleep
Page 8 Eerie Echoes
Page 10 Horrifying Heights
Page 12 Our Guest Star
Page 14 The Wicked Wide World
Page 16 A Tight Fit
Page 18 Home (Not So) Sweet Home
Page 20 Keep It Down!
Page 22 The Science of Fear
Page 24 Word Woe
Page 26 Hidden in the Closet
Page 28 Rotten Reflection
Page 30 Curtain Close
Page 31 Glossary
Page 32 Index

WELCOME TO THE SHOW!

We have all felt fear in our lives. But do you have a phobia? A phobia is a strong fear of something, such as spiders or flying.

> COME ONE, COME ALL! COME AND SEE SOME OF THE GREATEST FEARS KNOWN TO HUMANITY!

People have phobias of all sorts of things. Some people have phobias of things where there is no real danger.

The things you will see in our show were found all over the world. These are all real fears. Are you ready to find out what scares people the most?

Who knows, maybe you will leave the show with a brand-new phobia of your own?

CREEPY SLEEP

What is scarier than something you cannot escape? You cannot see it and you cannot stop it. It comes for you every night when you are alone in your bed.

You start to drift off, but your eyes snap open and you are wide awake again. It is an <u>invisible</u> monster that comes for you. That monster is called sleep.

The fear of sleep can affect people a lot. Sleep is very important to the human body, which means it is very difficult having this phobia.

It can make people very tired if they are scared to go to sleep. This means that people with a phobia of sleep might find it hard to do everyday things because they do not have the energy.

EERIE ECHOES

Do you hear that, that, that?

That is your echo bouncing off the walls of our tent. Look out and see how far it stretches. You must feel so small in here, here, here.

You might scream, but the echo will only scream back. You are all alone...

Certain types of space can trigger phobias in some people. You might have a phobia of empty houses, or open spaces such as fields.

You might even have a fear of voids. A void is an endless, empty place, such as outer space. Would being alone in the middle of nowhere scare you?

HORRIFYING HEIGHTS

Come with us to the top of the circus tent. Do not look down! Do not slip! It is a long way down to the bottom.

You do not want to fall but it is all you can think about this high up. You can feel your stomach turn. All it takes is one wrong foot...

How do you feel when you are high up? What is scarier? The fact that you are so high up, or that you might slip and fall all the way down? Scientists and doctors say these are different phobias, but it all feels the same when you are high up.

OUR GUEST STAR

Aretha Franklin was a famous musician from the US. She had an incredible singing voice. She released lots of albums and performed huge shows for lots of people.

Even as one of the biggest music stars in the world, Aretha Franklin had a phobia that affected her work.

In 1983, Aretha Franklin was on an aeroplane flying out of the city of Atlanta. The flight had a lot of turbulence, which means the aeroplane was shaken and thrown around by strong wind.

After that flight, Aretha never got on an aeroplane again. From then on, she travelled to her shows by bus and never performed outside of North America again.

THE WICKED WIDE WORLD

Come take a peek outside. You can see the wide world. The people, cars, buildings, everything! There is a lot going on, isn't there?

What if something bad happened out there? Would you be able to escape? What if you could not control what happened next? These sorts of <u>situations</u> where you cannot escape can trigger a phobia for some people.

Some people might have a phobia of crowds and busy places. They make them feel like they cannot get away. If a person's phobia of these situations is really bad, they might not be able to leave their homes.

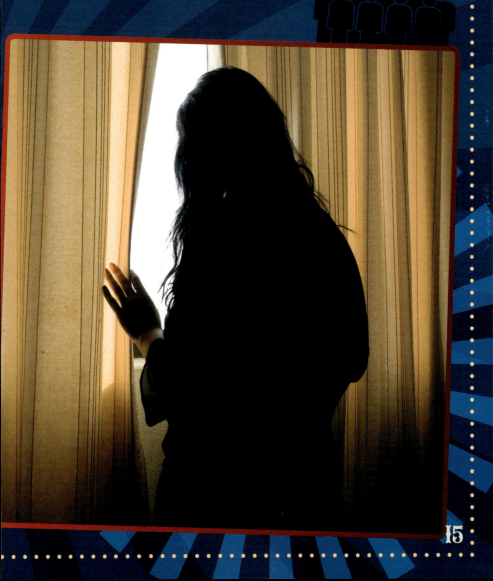

A TIGHT FIT

You are locked inside a small box. You barely fit. You cannot move. You are trapped. You can try and force your way out, but the box is shut tight. There is no way out.

Your breath becomes heavy. You start to sweat. This is how it feels to have a fear of small spaces.

People with a phobia of small spaces might take the stairs because they do not want to get in a lift. Sometimes, just closing a door can make a person feel trapped and a space feel tiny.

You can come out of the box for the rest of the show...

HOME (NOT SO) SWEET HOME

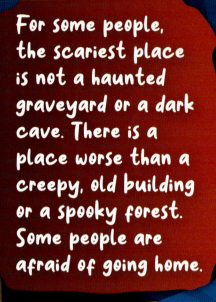

For some people, the scariest place is not a haunted graveyard or a dark cave. There is a place worse than a creepy, old building or a spooky forest. Some people are afraid of going home.

They might travel around the world and go to faraway places. When they think of going home, they feel scared.

Sometimes people get this phobia if something bad happened to them at home. Some people who spend a lot of time away from home, such as soldiers, might get this fear, too.

Some adults with this fear feel that going back home is a sign that they have not done well in the outside world.

KEEP IT DOWN!

For our next phobia, we need a telephone. It starts to ring. Louder and LOUDER. You can feel the RINGING in your ears, so loud that you cannot even think. You want the NOISE to stop more than anything.

You can feel it in your BONES, shaking your WHOLE BODY. You will do anything to MAKE IT STOP!

The fear of loud noises can be set off by any kind of sound, such as beeping cars, fireworks, music, people talking or anything loud.

For some people with this phobia, they find that putting their fingers in their ears and counting to 60 helps them calm down.

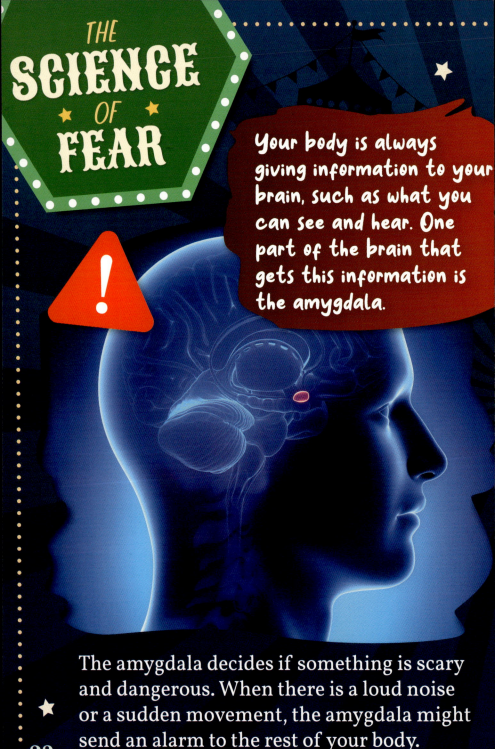

THE SCIENCE OF FEAR

Your body is always giving information to your brain, such as what you can see and hear. One part of the brain that gets this information is the amygdala.

The amygdala decides if something is scary and dangerous. When there is a loud noise or a sudden movement, the amygdala might send an alarm to the rest of your body.

The same information is also sent to the cortex. This is the part of the brain that thinks about the information. Are you really in danger?

If the cortex thinks you are safe, it will stop the alarm from the amygdala. This is why we might get <u>startled</u> for a second and calm down soon after.

WORD WOE

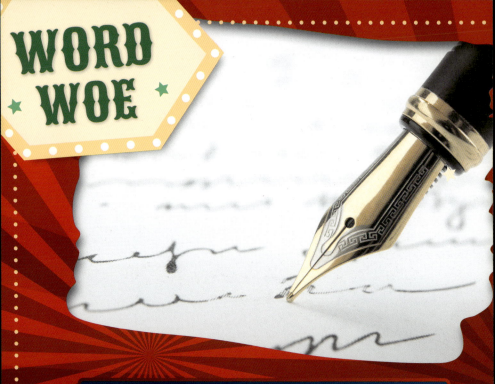

There once was a circus in town,
Where everyone left with a frown,
For it showed them their fears,
And left some in tears,
All without a creepy, evil clown.

For some people words are enough,
To make them feel afraid and rough.
Just a little rhyme,
With a bouncing **chime**,
Can fill their head with awful stuff.

Fearing a poem,
Has a long, difficult name.
Metrophobia.

For some it may start,
Reading pages and pages,
During school classes.

Words in verse,
Might terrify some,
On a page.

Read out loud,
It might make them scream,
And panic.

A poem,
Is all it takes,
To scare them.

HIDDEN IN THE CLOSET

It is time to look in the wardrobe. The wardrobe is tall, twice as big as you. The doors creak open, and clothes fall out on top of you.

The weight pins you down to the floor. The clothes start to wrap around you, feeling tight on your body. You are trapped inside them. This is what the fear of clothes feels like.

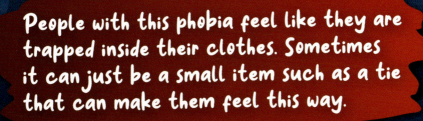

People with this phobia feel like they are trapped inside their clothes. Sometimes it can just be a small item such as a tie that can make them feel this way.

For some people, this phobia might have been caused by a very embarrassing or horrible moment involving clothes in their childhood.

ROTTEN REFLECTION

Bring out the mirror! It is time for the last fear in our show.

What happens when you look in a mirror? Are you seeing yourself, or are you looking into another world?

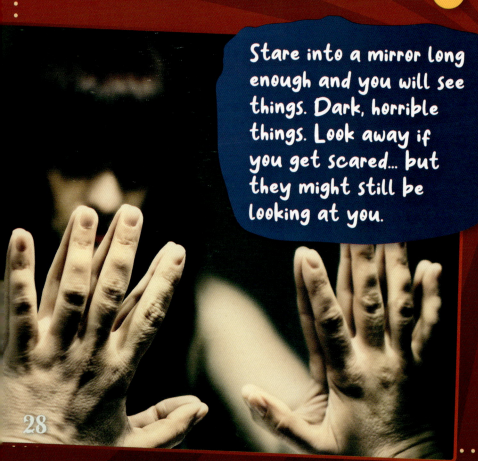

Stare into a mirror long enough and you will see things. Dark, horrible things. Look away if you get scared... but they might still be looking at you.

Some people are scared of mirrors because they believe in mysterious things outside of this world. These are called superstitions. Do you have any superstitions?

Some people think breaking a mirror can bring years of bad luck. That is even more to be worried about!

CURTAIN CLOSE

And that is our show! We hope you have enjoyed your journey through the phobias. Not everyone is able to get to the end.

We have seen a lot of phobias, but there are plenty more things to fear out in the world. Did you find something new to be afraid of? We hope you are brave enough to come again...

GLOSSARY

chime a ringing sound

invisible not able to be seen

situations all of the things happening that affect someone at a certain time

startled suddenly shocked or alarmed

INDEX

amygdala	22–23	heights	10
clothes	26–27	mirrors	28–29
echoes	8	noises	20–22
Franklin, Aretha	12–13	poems	25
		sleep	6–7

AN INTRODUCTION TO BOOKLIFE RAPID READERS...

Packed full of gripping topics and twisted tales, BookLife Rapid Readers are perfect for older children looking to propel their reading up to top speed. With three levels based on our planet's fastest animals, children will be able to find the perfect point from which to accelerate their reading journey. From the spooky to the silly, these roaring reads will turn every child at every reading level into a prolific page-turner!

CHEETAH
The fastest animals on land, cheetahs will be taking their first strides as they race to top speed.

MARLIN
The fastest animals under water, marlins will be blasting through their journey.

FALCON
The fastest animals in the air, falcons will be flying at top speed as they tear through the skies.